Who am I?

PHILIP BUNTING

Am I my name?

You have a name, but your name is not you. Your name is just a little bundle of letters. You by any other name would still be you! These vowels and consonants will not determine who you are, or who you will be. Yet somebody who loves you chose your name, so hold it close!

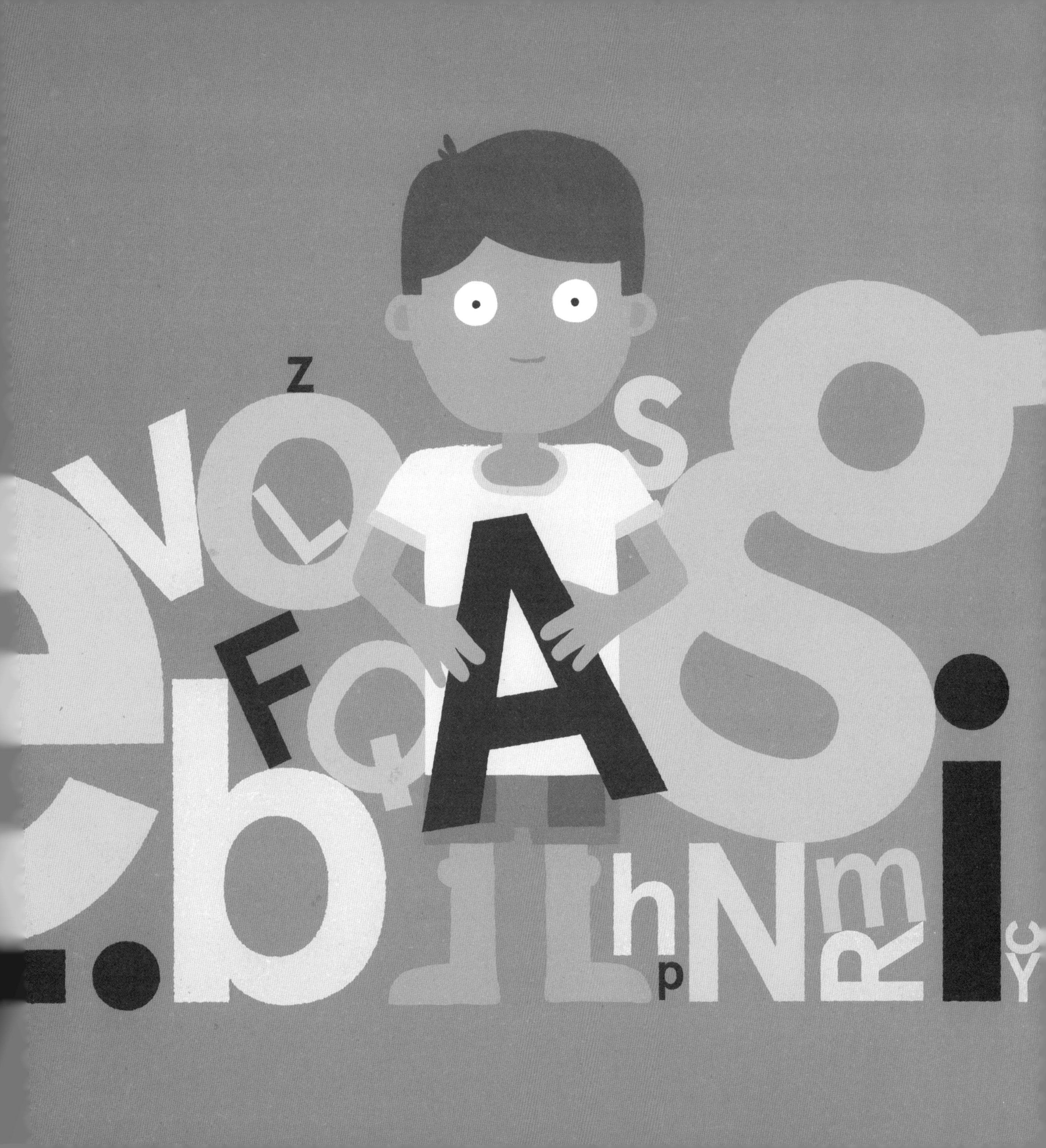

Am I where I'm from?

Where you are from might give you a preference for sushi over spaghetti, and a way of speaking, or dressing. But no matter where on Earth you're from, we are all creatures of the same planet, sailing around the same star, looking up at the same moon. Towns and cities will come and go, nations and borders are all made up! The place you are from is the Earth, just like everyone else.

Am I my stuff?

Your possessions can help you do great things and share fun times with others, but your stuff will never make you who you are. The things you own will change as you get bigger, so share your stuff and learn to let it go. And as you grow, you will begin to find that the more you know, the less you'll need.

Am I my gender?

You are much more than your gender.
How you were born does not define
who you are — or who you will be.
Girls, boys and everyone in between,
we are all a part of the same whole.
We are all just people, and all people
are equal.

Am I the colour of my skin?

Your skin is your spacesuit on your voyage through the present, as we circle around our sun. They come in all colours, but the colour of yours does not make you who you are. Your skin keeps all the good stuff in, and the nasty things out! We wouldn't last long without our spacesuits, so take great care of yours, and be proud of its beautiful colour.

So if I'm not my skin, am I my muscles?

Your muscles are a marvellous part of your body, but they do not make you who you are (no matter how beefy you become). Your muscles will take you places near and far. Exercise them often and keep them strong!

Frontalis

Temporalis

Tiny, tiny hand
muscles (various)

Biceps

~~Brachiosaurus~~
Brachioradialis

Pectorals

Triceps

Abdominal
muscles

Obliques

Quadriceps

Hamstrings
(inside)

Unsolicited medical advice:
If your knees are this
knobbly, consult a
physician, post haste!

Calf muscles
(inside)

Tibialis

Foot muscles
(various)

OK then, am I my bones?

Your skeleton helps to keep you upright, and keeps your insides safe. Without them bones, your body would be like a big, mushy bag of warm soup, lolloping around the place like a beached jellyfish. Your bones do not make you who you are (but remember to brush your teeth twice each day, unless you really like eating soup).

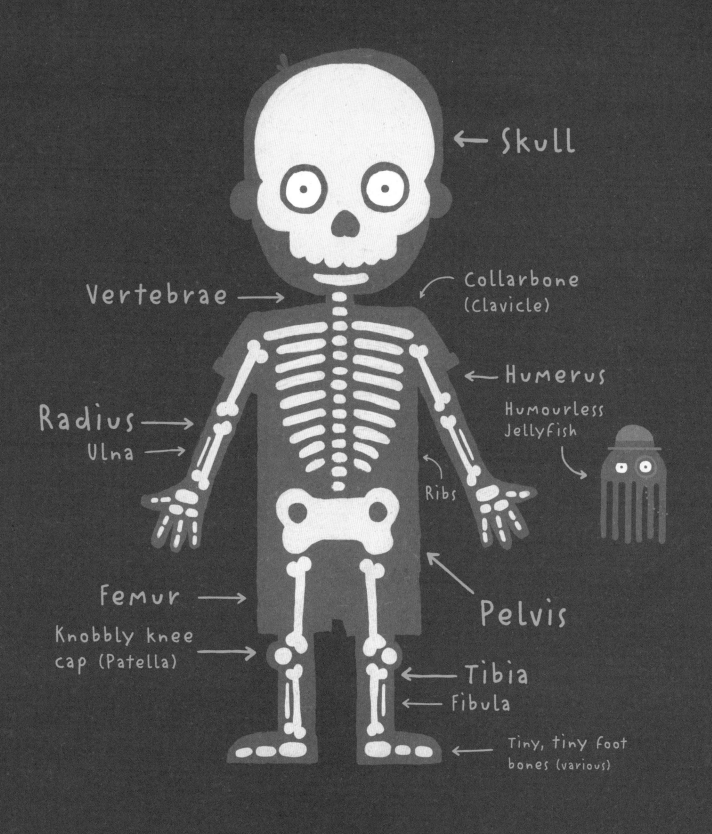

How about my guts and stuff?

They're not you either. But all of these bits and pieces very kindly keep your body ticking over. Give your insides plenty of good food, eat mostly plants and not too many treats. Drink lots of water, and breathe deeply. If you look after your insides, your insides will look after you.

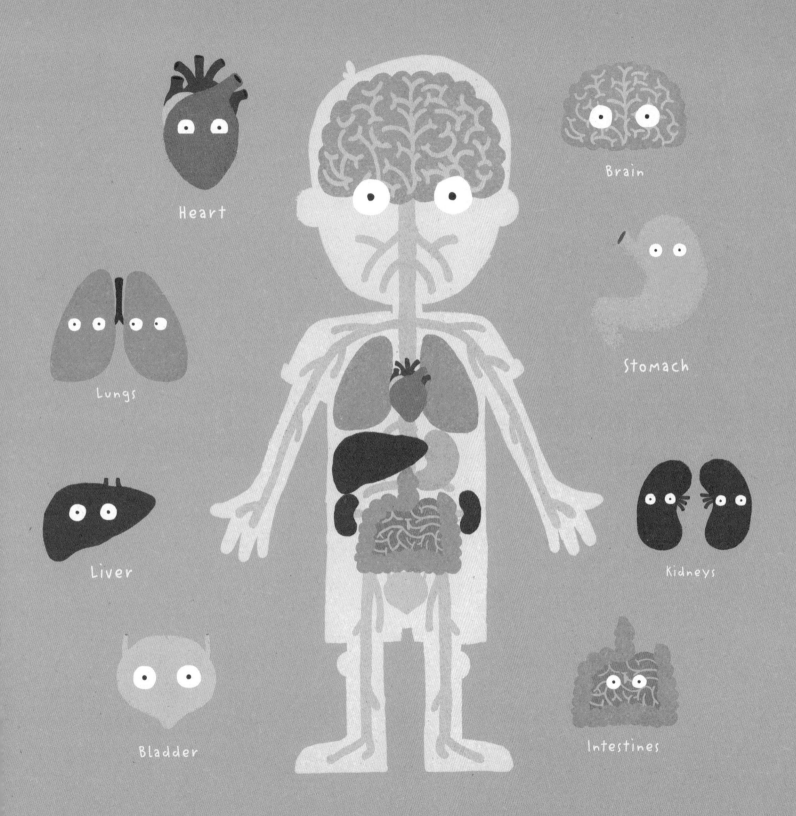

Heart

Brain

Lungs

Stomach

Liver

Kidneys

Bladder

Intestines

Very serious disclaimer: Despite appearances, only one of these organs maintains consciousness. And it's not the bladder.

Am I my senses?

Your senses are a multitude of very
handy little bodily systems. They cleverly
convert objects from the outside world
into information that your brain can
understand, via tiny electrical impulses:
"Too cold! Ouch! Oh, that really smells ..."
They are very useful indeed — helping
to keep you happy, healthy and safe —
but your senses do not make you
who you are.

Am I my thoughts?

You and you alone see your thoughts. These are just ideas and memories passing through your mind. You are not the thoughts themselves, and you can change them if you try. Hold the good thoughts close and let the bad ones go. Your mind will take you much further than your body ever will, so feed your mind with new things every day. Be kind to your mind, give it lots of rest and lots of play.

Am I my feelings?

Your feelings, emotions and instincts are
just like thoughts, but they come from
a much deeper place in your mind.
Your emotions can teach you lots
of things that thoughts cannot.
So learn from them, trust them,
but just like thoughts, remember
to let the bad ones go.

Now we are getting closer
to who you are ...

So, if I'm not
my name
my place
my stuff
my gender
my skin colour
my muscles
my bones
my guts and stuff
my senses
my thoughts, or
my feelings ...

Who am I?

Well, all of these things are the makings of you, but your true self is so much greater than any of these bits and pieces.

Right now, you are one tiny human (one of eight billion or thereabouts) bobbing along through the multiverse on this wonderful little spaceship we call the Earth.

You and your fellow travellers are from the same place, and are made of the same stuff. We all share the same hope, fear, joy and love. We all exist as individual people, yet we are deeply connected, far beyond the limits of our bodies, minds and borders.

We are all one. But who are you?

Pootling around, somewhere behind your eyes, is the thing that makes you, you. Your truest self. This part of you is pretty mysterious. We all know it is there but we can't seem to agree what it is, where it comes from or what to call it. Some call it the soul, some call it the psyche, others call it Atman.

Whatever you choose to call it, this is the part of you that sees what you see, wonders what you wonder, and feels what you feel. This part of you has always been here, and always will be.

That is who you are.

But who you will choose
to be in this lifetime ...
well, that is up to you.

F O R L A U R A X X

"We are all one consciousness
experiencing itself subjectively."
Bill Hicks

First published in 2020 by Omnibus Books
An imprint of Scholastic Australia Pty Limited

This edition published in 2021 by Scholastic Children's Books
Euston House, 24 Eversholt Street
London, NW1 1DB
A division of Scholastic Ltd
www.scholastic.co.uk

London – New York – Toronto – Sydney – Auckland
Mexico City – New Delhi – Hong Kong

Text copyright © Philip Bunting, 2020
Illustrations copyright © Philip Bunting, 2020

ISBN 978 0702 30770 6

Acknowledgement of Country: I would like to acknowledge the traditional custodians of the land on which
I live and work, and I pay respect to the Gubbi Gubbi nation. I pay respects to the Elders of the community
and extend my recognition to their descendants. Philip Bunting.